This book is for Ezzy & Leena.

If being your mom is everything God has for me in this life, it will be a life well lived!

And thank you to my best friend, husband and partner in everything. Every gift in my life started with you.

I love you three so much it hurts!

XOXO

Once upon a time

...a time before time. When nothing existed.

Nothing that is but a powerful king.

A king who alone would make everything!
All of the world and everything in it.
Sound like a good story?

Okay, let's begin it.

He dreamed up His people, whom He'd love and adore.
He quietly pictured who He'd do it all for.
Then with that vision held dear in His heart,
He decided His dream was ready to start.

"Let there be light above to shine down on their faces.
To hold them with warmth in my loving, good graces."

He made for them animals, loving and smart.
Some good for food and some good for the heart.

He made for them rain, to dance in and play.

To water their crops in the heat of the day.

He made big things and small things.
He made summer, spring, winter and fall.
Then smiled and said, "Now for the best of them all..."

He made His people. He loved them.
He walked with them day after day.
But it didn't take long before they started to stray.
The snake and the apple, that's a different story.
But basically His people fell from His Glory.

Years went by since our story's start
and time didn't help the state of their heart.
The King watched confused as they'd bow to a cow.
They'd pray to the rain as they farmed with their plow.

"What are they doing? How could this be?
These things that they praise were all made by me!
Why worship a cow when it's just a creation?"
He looked for those who still loved Him, filled with frustration.

He found a group still drawn to His light.
He told them "For my Kingdom, be ready to fight."

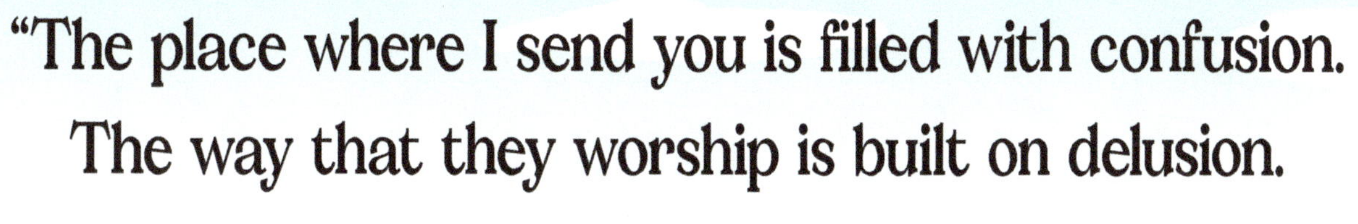

"The place where I send you is filled with confusion.
The way that they worship is built on delusion.

When you go to this place, don't take what you see
and then try to apply it in worship to me."

Deuteronomy 12:30-31

SOL INVICTVS

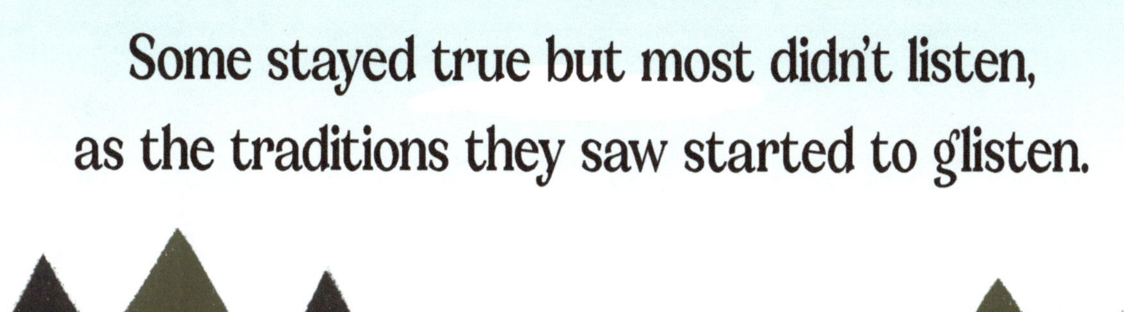

Some stayed true but most didn't listen,
as the traditions they saw started to glisten.

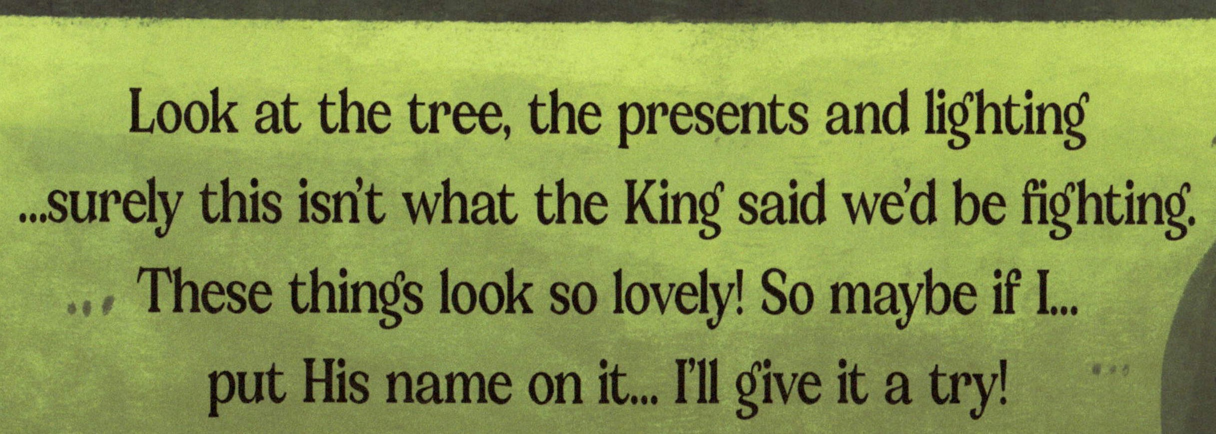

Look at the tree, the presents and lighting
...surely this isn't what the King said we'd be fighting.
These things look so lovely! So maybe if I...
put His name on it... I'll give it a try!

But the King wasn't fooled, He knew just what they'd done.
They weren't worshiping Him, they worshiped the sun.
The things that they did, the traditions they'd start,
only appeared to have Him placed at the heart.

“My people, my children! Why can't you see,
you're so lost in the sin of idolatry.
For anything you put above me in your heart,
takes you further from the glorious plan I had at the start.”

"So come, let me lead you back to the garden.
For *I* designed special days for you to take part in.

They worship what's made but you know the Maker.
So don't settle for a likeness, a knock off, or faker.
I love you, I made you. I want you to see,
the wonderful plan that leads you...

...back to Me.

There's nothing more special than knowing The Maker, the God of Heaven and Earth! God loves knowing us and being known by us. Because of that He gave us seven special Holy days, designed to show us the way back to His perfect garden.

Passover

Feast of Unleavened Bread

Pentecost

Feast of Trumpets

Day of Atonement

Feast of Tabernacles

The Last Great Day

PASSOVER

The Maker sent His Son to die and take our punishment for doing wrong.

FEAST OF UNLEAVENED BREAD

The Maker teaches us it's important to obey His rules, but it's very hard to do it on our own.

PENTECOST

The Maker gives us His Holy Spirit to live in us and help us to obey the rules.

FEAST OF TRUMPETS

The Maker sends His Son back to the earth to save us.

DAY OF ATONEMENT

The Maker restores His people to the perfection they had in the garden.

FEAST OF TABERNACLES

The Maker's Son rules, making all the earth like the Garden of Eden.

THE LAST GREAT DAY

The Maker judges all those that chose their own way over the beauty of life lived His way in the garden.

author.iknowthemaker@gmail.com

Printed in The United States of America
ISBN 979-8-218-15813-2

Illustrations by Vikkireds

www.ingramcontent.com/pod-product-compliance
Lightning Source LLC
LaVergne TN
LVHW071211160826
845679LV00003B/801

9798218158132